What kind of animal is Pat?	☐ horse ☐ cat
What does she like to do?	☐ run ☐ swim
What can Pat do?	☐ jump ☐ walk

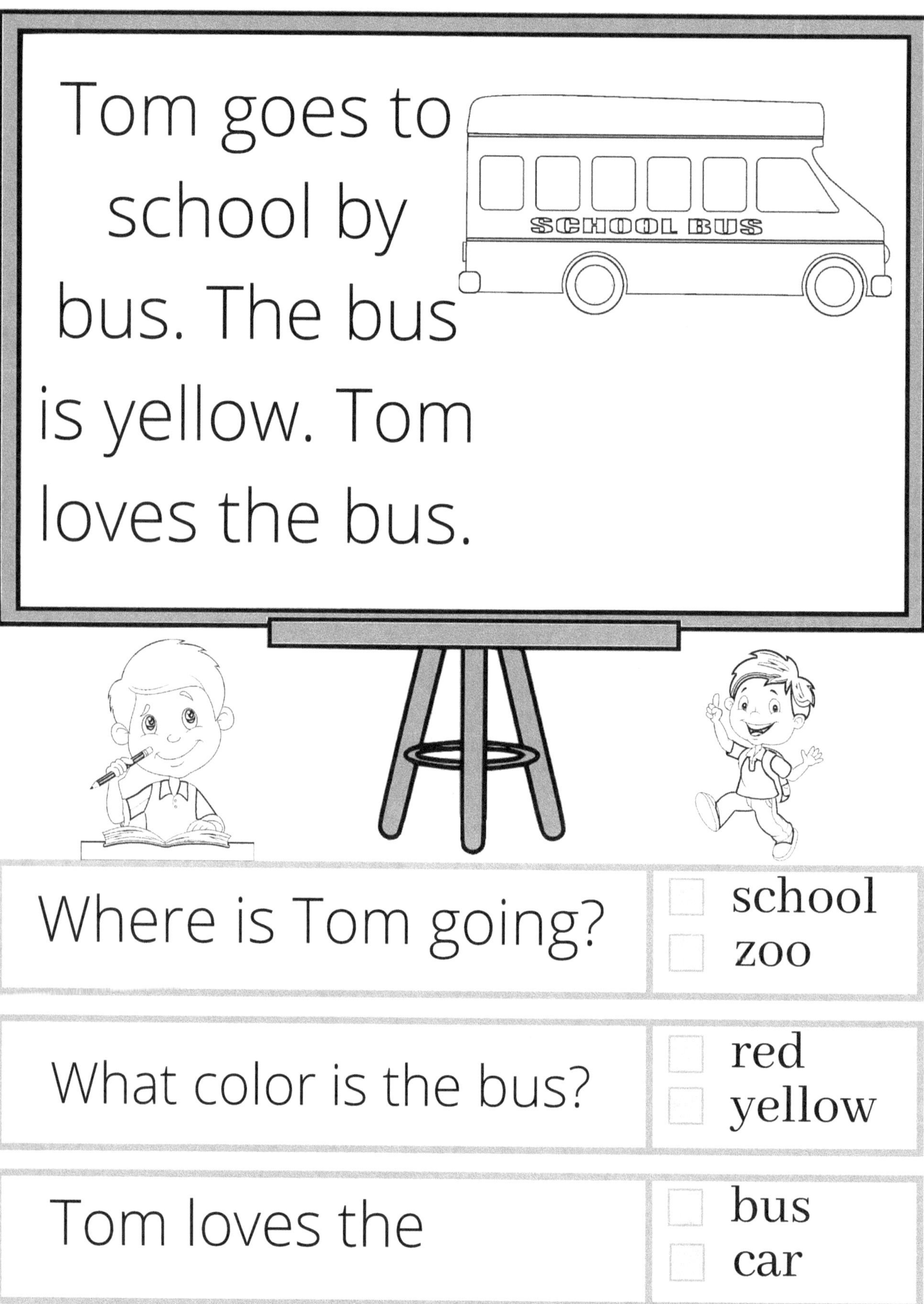

Where is Tom going?	☐ school ☐ zoo
What color is the bus?	☐ red ☐ yellow
Tom loves the	☐ bus ☐ car

The cow likes to eat	☐ hay ☐ banana
What color is the cow?	☐ green ☐ white
The cow lives on the	☐ house ☐ farm

The bunny likes to eat — ☐ carrot / ☐ meat

The bunny hops from the — ☐ trees / ☐ car

The bunny lives on the — ☐ house / ☐ farm

Who has a balloon?	☐ Sofia ☐ sister
Who will she give it to?	☐ Tom ☐ sister
What color is it?	☐ orange ☐ red

My name is
James, I have
a black bag, I
am going to
work

My name is	☐ Tom ☐ James
What color is the bag?	☐ pink ☐ black
James goes to	☐ work ☐ school

What do you see?
seal
fish

What color is the seal?
white
green

Where is the seal?
beach
garden

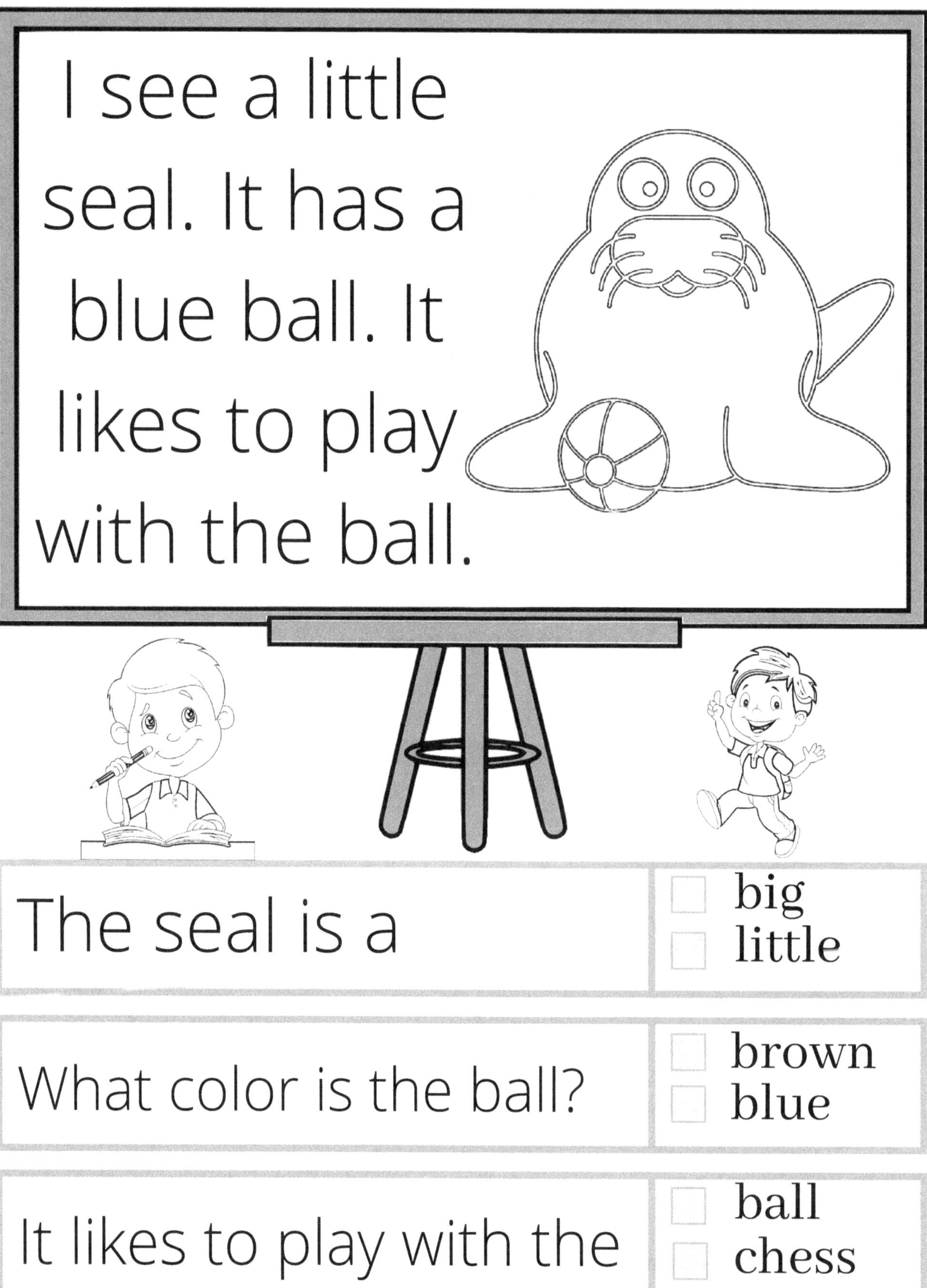

The seal is a

- [ ] big
- [ ] little

What color is the ball?

- [ ] brown
- [ ] blue

It likes to play with the

- [ ] ball
- [ ] chess

Jerry is a dog.
He has black
fur. He loves
to chase his
red ball in
the garden.

What kind of animal is Jerry?	☐ mouse ☐ dog
What color is the ball?	☐ red ☐ blue
What does the dog like to do in the garden?	☐ chase ball ☐ sleep

What is my name?

Lara
Olivia

What do I have?

dog
cat

How old is it?

five
six

What color is the hen?

- [ ] orange
- [ ] red

How do hens lay eggs?

- [ ] one
- [ ] four

A hen is a female?

- [ ] yes
- [ ] no

How does a bird feel?

☐ happy
☐ hungry

What did the bird catch?

☐ worm
☐ snake

The worm is a

☐ small
☐ big

The bat eats
- insects
- human

The bat flies at
- day
- night

What color is the bat?
- black
- pink

My friend is	☐ Lucas ☐ Tom
What did I give him?	☐ cherry ☐ apple
What color was it?	☐ blue ☐ red

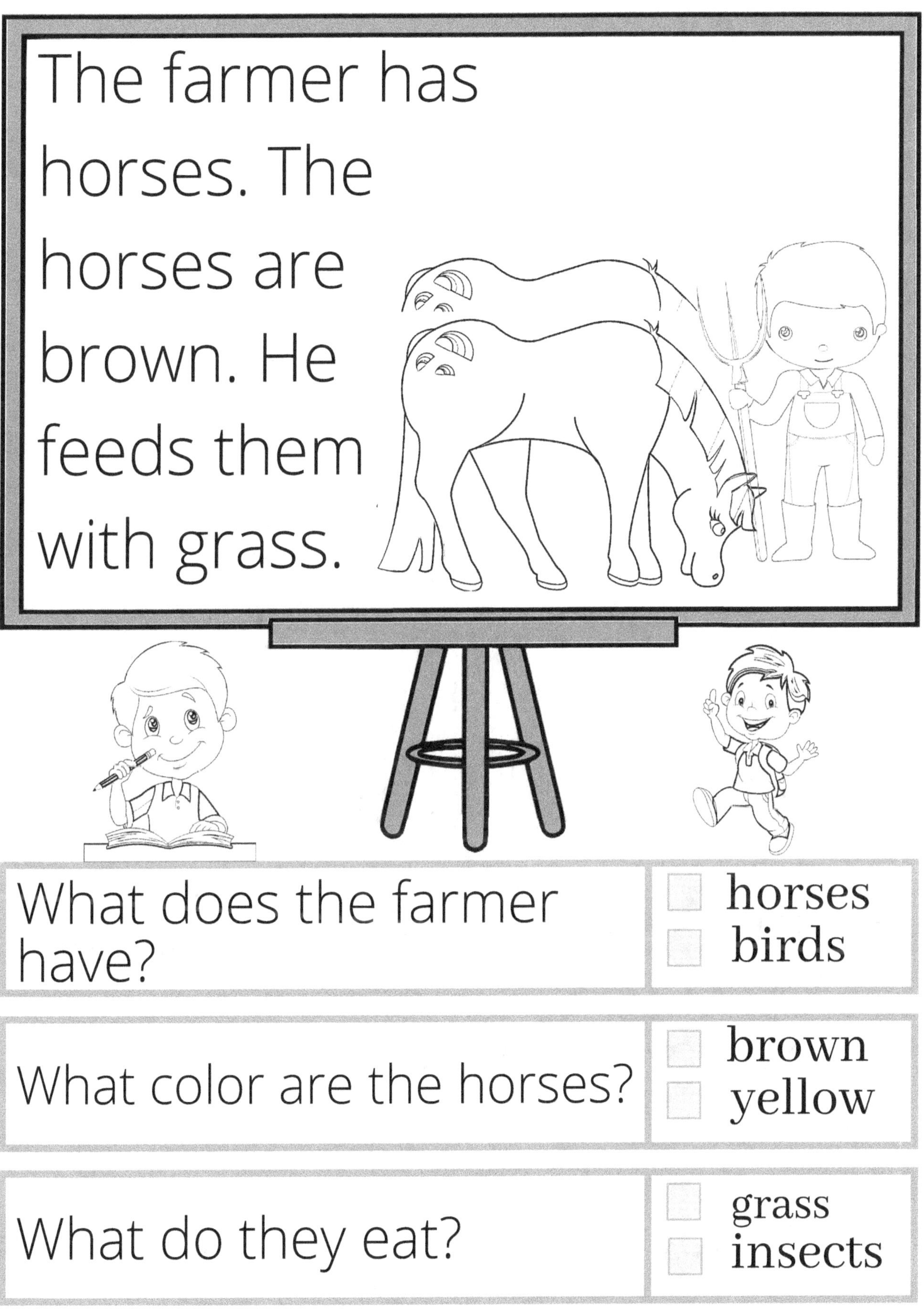

The farmer has horses. The horses are brown. He feeds them with grass.
What does the farmer have?
horses
birds
What color are the horses?
brown
yellow
What do they eat?
grass
insects

Noah and Oliver are men. They love horses. They have four horse on the farm.

Noah and Oliver are	☐ men ☐ women
How many horses do they have?	☐ two ☐ four
What do they love?	☐ sheep ☐ horses

I see the rocket. The rocket can fly fast. It is going to the moon.

What do you see?	☐ car ☐ rocket
The rocket can fly	☐ fast ☐ slowly
The rocket goes to	☐ moon ☐ sun

What do you see?	☐ Lion ☐ camel
What does eat the lion?	☐ grass ☐ meat
What color is the lion?	☐ brown ☐ white

The whale is	☐ blue ☐ green
The whale is	☐ small ☐ big
The whale lives in the	☐ house ☐ sea

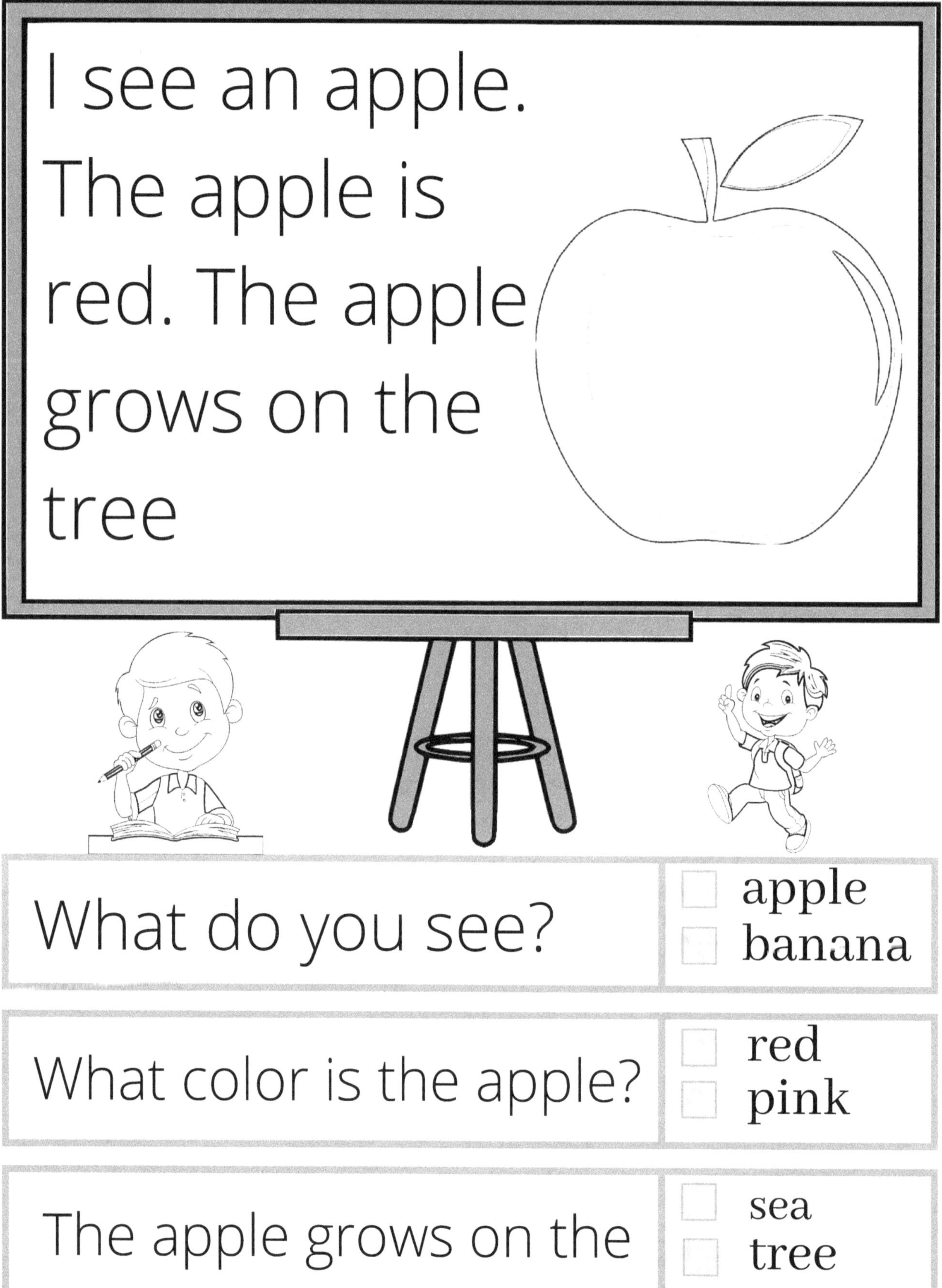

I see an apple. The apple is red. The apple grows on the tree
What do you see?
apple
banana
What color is the apple?
red
pink
The apple grows on the
sea
tree

Ant is a very small insect that lives in the colony.
Most ants in a colony are female workers.

What kind of animal is an ant?	☐ insect ☐ monkey
Ants live in a	☐ colony ☐ sea
Most ants are female	☐ queens ☐ workers

The moon is yellow. The moon rises in the sky at night and moves around the earth.

What color is the moon?	☐ pink ☐ yellow
What time does the moon rise?	☐ night ☐ day
The moon moves around the	☐ earth ☐ sun

I see a long banana, It has yellow skin. The monkey eats the banana.

What do you see?	☐ banana ☐ pear
What color is the banana?	☐ yellow ☐ Beige
The monkey eats the	☐ meat ☐ banana

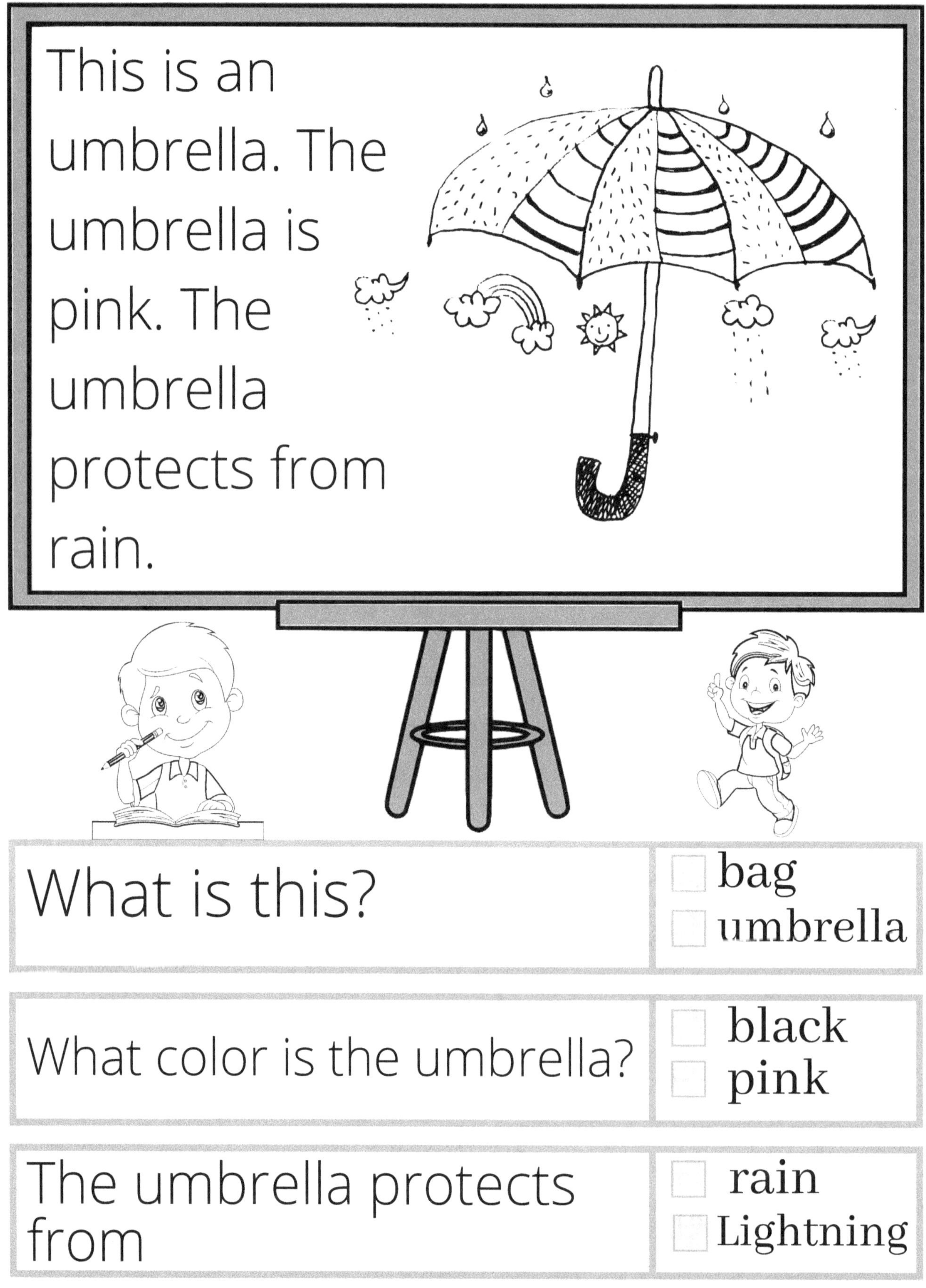

What is this?

☐ bag
☐ umbrella

What color is the umbrella?

☐ black
☐ pink

The umbrella protects from

☐ rain
☐ Lightning

Jack bought a new hat. The hat is purple. He loves hats.

Jack bought a	☐ hat ☐ jacket
What color is the hat?	☐ purple ☐ red
What does love Jack?	☐ hat ☐ bird

William has a
blue ball. William
plays football
with his friends.
William loves
football.

William plays	☐ Volleyball ☐ football
What color is the ball?	☐ green ☐ blue
What does love William?	☐ football ☐ Tennis

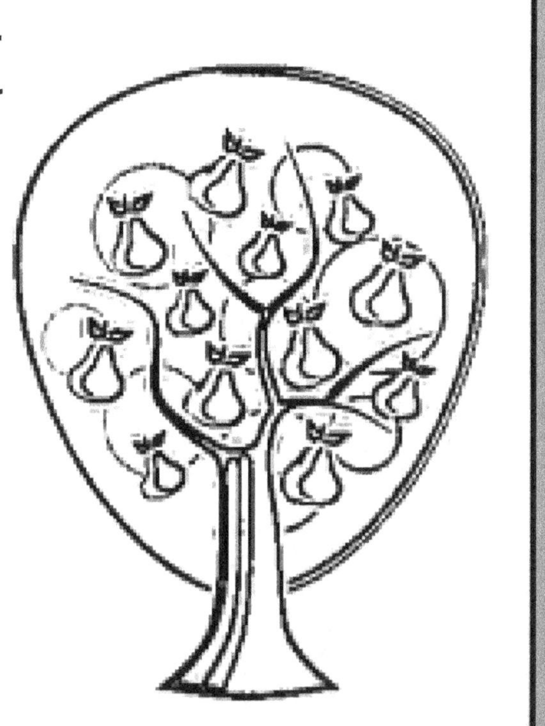

I see a tree. It has yellow pears on it. I like to eat a pear.

What do you see?	☐ tree ☐ house
What is on the tree?	☐ banana ☐ pear
What color are the pears?	☐ yellow ☐ red

What is my friend's name?

- [ ] Tom
- [ ] John

We like to

- [ ] read
- [ ] swim

We read books in

- [ ] library
- [ ] house

Jack is five yours old and lives with his family in a big house near the beach.

Jack lives with his

- ☐ family
- ☐ Friend

The house where Jack lives is

- ☐ small
- ☐ big

Jack's house is near the

- ☐ city
- ☐ beach

The frog lives in the
☐ nest
☐ pond

He jumps on a
☐ tree
☐ log

The frog eats
☐ insects
☐ fruits

My name is Jack. I am twenty-eight yours old. I am a doctor.

Who I am?	☐ Jack ☐ Franck
I am a	☐ doctor ☐ farmer
How old I am?	☐ 28 ☐ 25

Who I am?	joseph Michael
I am an	Clown engineer
How old I am?	23 25

This girl has
a cat. The
cat is white.
The cat eats
a mouse.

What does the girl has?	☐ cat ☐ mouse
What color is the cat?	☐ black ☐ white
The cat eats a	☐ mouse ☐ grass

I have a brother.
His name is
Henry. He likes
to play tennis.
He plays tennis
every Sunday.

What is my brother's name?	☐ Henry ☐ Aiden

He likes to play	☐ chess ☐ tennis

He plays every	☐ day ☐ Sunday

Who likes to ride the horse?	☐ Carter ☐ David
What color is the horse?	☐ green ☐ brown
David rides in the	☐ morning ☐ noon

Sara has		☐ flowers ☐ trees
Her flowers are in the		☐ pot ☐ plat
Her flowers are		☐ pink ☐ red

Where did Lucas go yesterday?	☐ School ☐ zoo
Which animal did he see?	☐ giraffe ☐ monkey
What color is the lion?	☐ brown ☐ red

I am going to
the beach
with my
family. We are
going to
swim.

Where I am going?	☐ beach ☐ hotel
What we will do?	☐ swim ☐ run
I am going with my	☐ family ☐ friend

What do you see?	☐ hen ☐ turkey
What color are his feathers?	☐ brown ☐ blue
How many wings does he have?	☐ two ☐ four

The boy likes to	☐ paint ☐ color
The boy can paint a	☐ cat ☐ dog
His friend can paint	☐ forest ☐ flowers

The girl likes the	☐ rain ☐ snow
What color is the umbrella?	☐ pink ☐ yellow
What does she love the girl?	☐ play ☐ winter

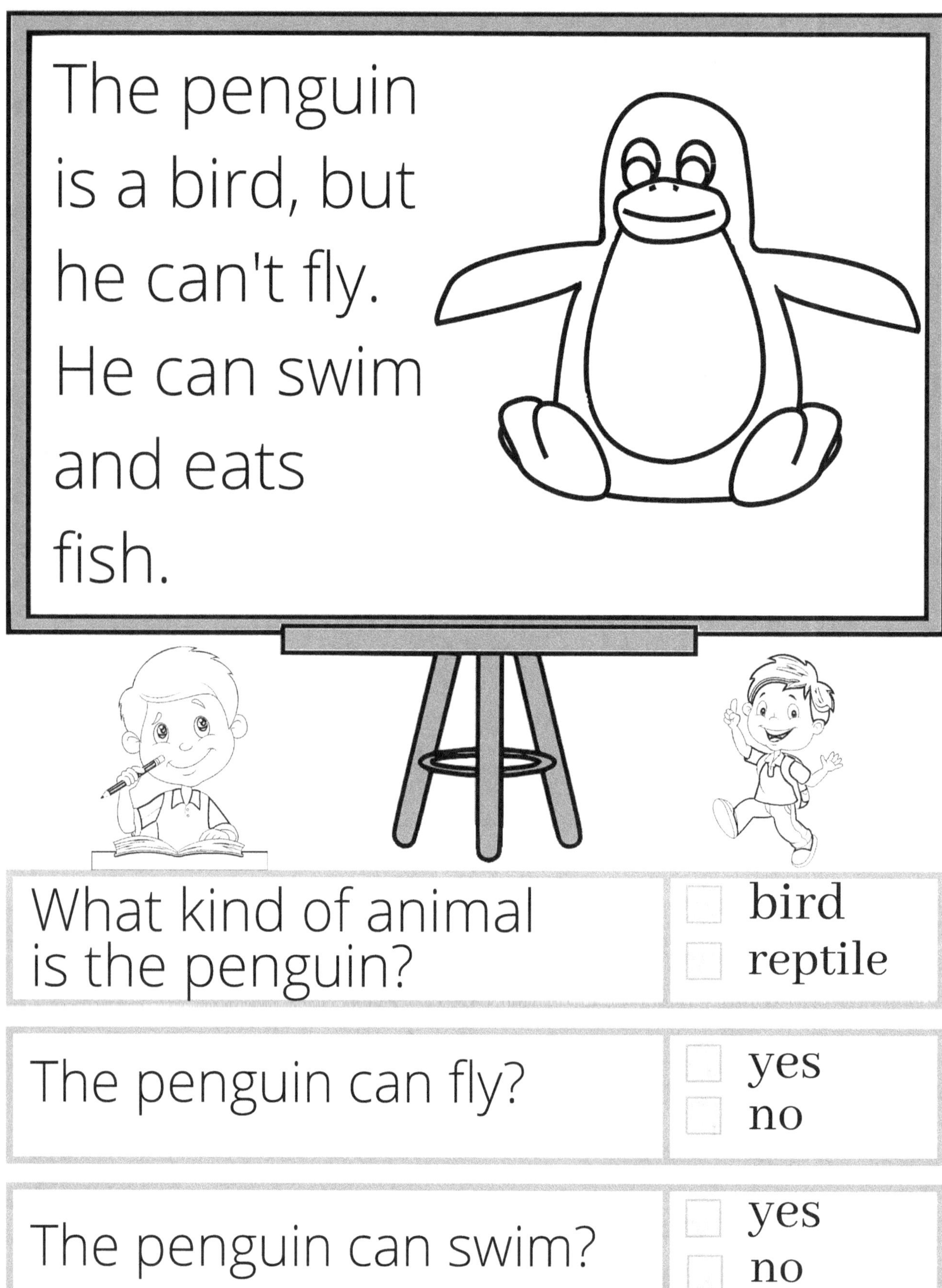

What kind of animal is the penguin?	☐ bird ☐ reptile
The penguin can fly?	☐ yes ☐ no
The penguin can swim?	☐ yes ☐ no

What color is the fox?	☐ white ☐ brown
The fox runs	☐ fast ☐ slowly
What does like the fox?	☐ sleep ☐ wag tail

The bees love	☐ flowers ☐ tree

Where he lives the bees?	☐ hive ☐ house

What does make the bees?	☐ honey ☐ water

What kind of animal is Sam?	☐ dog ☐ camel
What is my dog's name?	☐ Oliver ☐ Sam
I play with	☐ Lara ☐ Sam

The elephants are	☐ big ☐ small

The elephants live in	☐ Asia ☐ America

What do they eat?	☐ meat ☐ plants

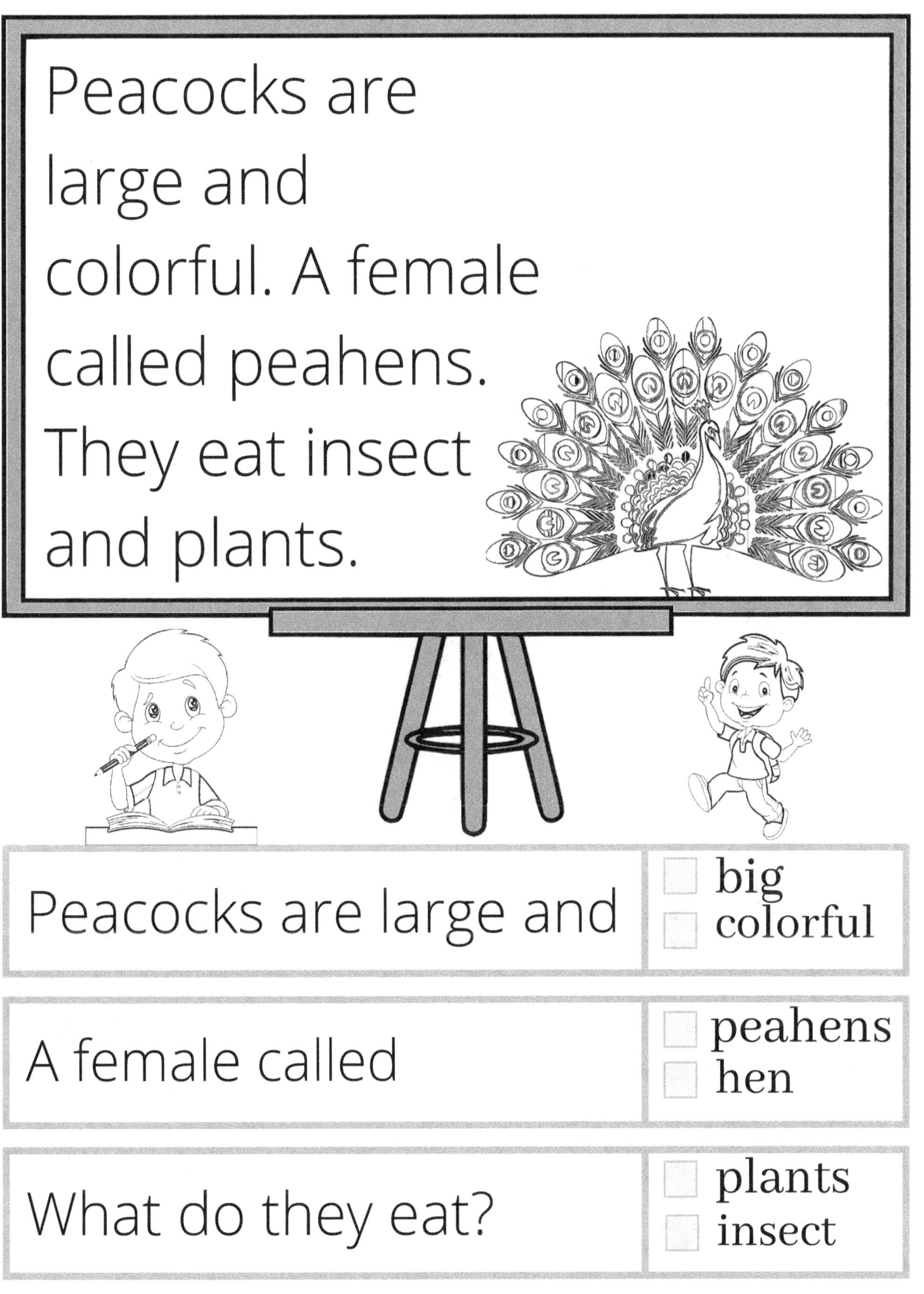

Peacocks are large and

- [ ] big
- [ ] colorful

A female called

- [ ] peahens
- [ ] hen

What do they eat?

- [ ] plants
- [ ] insect

What do you see?
☐ donkey
☐ bunny

What he has?
☐ basket
☐ carrot

I see four
☐ eggs
☐ bunny

What color are the pumpkins?	☐ red ☐ orange
Pumpkins are	☐ big ☐ small
Pumpkins are	☐ round ☐ black

What do you see?	☐ owl ☐ cat
What color is the owl?	☐ pink ☐ brown
The owl has big	☐ eyes ☐ body